Study Guide

Business Communication

THIRD EDITION

Tom Means

Contributing Author

Victoria Hathaway

CENGAGE

Australia • Brazil • Mexico • Singapore • United Kingdom • United States

ISBN: 978-1-337-40392-4

Cengage
20 Channel Center Street
Boston, MA 02210
USA

Cengage is a leading provider of customized learning solutions with employees residing in nearly 40 different countries and sales in more than125 countries around the world. Find your local representative at: **www.cengage.com**.

Cengage products are represented in Canada by Nelson Education, Ltd.

To learn more about Cengage platforms and services, visit **www.cengage.com**.

For your course and learning solutions, visit **ngl.cengage.com/school**.

Printed in the United States of America
Print Number: 01   Print Year: 2018

Table of Contents

Chapter 1
Communication in Your Life

A. Key Terms

Directions: Write the letter of the definition that matches the word beside each word.

_____   1.   channel   a.   A person who creates and shares a message

_____   2.   communication barrier   b.   A positive feeling or attitude toward others

_____   3.   feedback   c.   A communication that is written, spoken, or signaled

_____   4.   goodwill   d.   Words used in a spoken message

_____   5.   message   e.   The mode used to send a message, such as a letter or speaking to someone

_____   6.   receiver   f.   A thing or condition that interferes with communication

_____   7.   sender   g.   The response of a receiver to a message, such as a comment or a nod of the head

_____   8.   verbal message   h.   A person who hears or reads and interprets a message

B. Purposes of Communication

Directions: List the purposes of business communication and give examples of each.

   Purposes   **Examples**

1.   _____   _____

   _____   _____

2.   _____   _____

   _____   _____

3.   _____   _____

   _____   _____

4.   _____   _____

   _____   _____

C. Types of Business Communication

Directions: For each situation described, indicate whether the communication is formal or informal and whether it is upward, downward, or lateral communication.

1. You send an email to a coworker wishing her a happy birthday.

   _____

2. Your manager sends a letter to all department employees that explains a new overtime policy.

   _____

3. The company president speaks to a group of employees regarding improving sales.

   _____

4. You mention to your boss during lunch that company morale seems low.

   _____

5. You send an email to a worker in another department requesting information needed to complete a report.

   _____

D. Elements of the Communication Process

Directions: For each situation, indicate the element of the communication process that is described.

1. The text of a letter

   _____

2. A person speaking at a meeting

   _____

3. A group of people listening to a speech

   _____

4. A response to a comment made by a speaker

   _____

5. A telephone call

   _____

E. Communication Barriers

Directions: For each situation, identify the communication barrier. Indicate whether the barrier is internal or external.

1. The students in Mrs. Robert's classroom are having trouble hearing her lecture because of construction noise in the street nearby.

   _____

   _____

2. Maria is reading a chapter from her history book. The hour is late, and she is having trouble staying awake.

   _____

   _____

3. Members of the Marketing Department are listening to plans for a new advertising campaign. The room is very warm, making everyone uncomfortable.

   _____

   _____

4. Gloria is listening to a class discussion about zoology. She is bored and not at all interested in the topic being discussed. She wanted to take a different class, but that class was already filled.

   _____

   _____

F. Message Environment

Directions: Answer the following questions about message environment.

1. What is a message environment?

   _____

   _____

2. Why is being aware of the message environment important?

   _____

   _____

3. What points should you consider when selecting a physical location where you will speak to listeners?

   _____

   _____

   _____

G. Audience Analysis

Directions: You have been asked to speak to the members of your local school board regarding an event that students would like to hold. Decide what the event will be. For example, the event might be a dance or a sporting event. Complete an audience analysis by answering the following questions.

- Who are the receivers? What are their genders and ages?

  _____

  _____

- Have I interacted with these receivers before? If so, what is our relationship?

  _____

  _____

- Do the receivers have experience or education that relates to the topic of the message?

  _____

  _____

- What are the concerns and needs of the receivers?

  _____

  _____

- Do the receivers have a particular motive in this situation?

  _____

  _____

- What are the beliefs, biases, values, and viewpoints of the receivers?

  _____

  _____

- What ideas, if any, can be used to communicate effectively with the receivers?

  _____

  _____

- How will the message affect the receivers? Will the message make the receivers happy? Sad? Pleased? Upset?

  _____

  _____

H. Reading on the Job

In most cases, you will be required to spend time reading while on the job. Identify five instances where reading is important and could enhance your ability to obtain upward mobility. Give examples of each reason for reading in the workplace.

1. _____
   _____
   _____
   _____
   _____

2. _____
   _____
   _____
   _____
   _____

3. _____
   _____
   _____
   _____
   _____

4. _____
   _____
   _____
   _____
   _____

5. _____
   _____
   _____
   _____
   _____

I. Improving Reading Skills

Directions: Answer the following questions about reading skills.

1. Are effective reading skills important for success on the job? Why or why not?

   _____

   _____

2. What are the three basic types of reading? Is the same reading speed appropriate for each type? Why or why not?

   _____

   _____

   _____

3. What is the average speed at which many people read? At what speed do exceptional readers read?

   _____

   _____

4. Is reading speed more important than comprehension? Explain your answer.

   _____

   _____

5. What tips can you follow to improve reading speed and comprehension?

   _____

   _____

   _____

   _____

   _____

   _____

   _____

   _____

   _____

   _____

   _____

   _____

   _____

   _____

Chapter 2
Diversity and Ethics

A. Key Terms

Directions: Write the letter of the definition that matches the word beside each word.

_____	1. culture	a.	The presence of a wide range of variation in qualities or attributes of people or things
_____	2. diversity	b.	A set of rules of behavior for a particular place or situation
_____	3. ethics	c.	The act of claiming someone else's words or ideas as your own
_____	4. etiquette	d.	A bias that prevents objective thought about a person or thing
_____	5. globalization	e.	A set of beliefs, attitudes, practices, and social customs that distinguishes a group of people
_____	6. plagiarism	f.	An oversimplified belief about a group of people
_____	7. prejudice	g.	Principles of right and wrong that govern behavior
_____	8. stereotype	h.	The integration of activities among nations in areas such as commerce and culture

B. Culture and Communication

Directions: Answer each question in the space provided.

1. What is diversity?

   _____

   _____

2. Why is the American workplace likely to become increasingly multicultural?

   _____

   _____

3. How will the continuing development of a global workplace affect American workers?

   _____

   _____

4. How can cultural differences become communication barriers?

   _____

   _____

5. Why is body language important when communicating across cultures?

_____

_____

6. Tom and Ramon are having a conversation in the hallway. What may happen if Tom has a smaller area of personal space than Ramon?

_____

_____

7. What is cross-cultural communication?

_____

_____

8. How can learning about another culture aid cross-cultural communication?

_____

_____

9. Why might holidays be a sensitive issue for a coworker from another country?

_____

_____

10. Why should you avoid using slang and jargon when communicating with someone whose first language is not English?

_____

_____

11. What types of diversity, other than cultural, might an American worker encounter in the workplace?

_____

_____

12. Why might a sentence that begins in the following manner offend a coworker?

"People of your background usually…."

_____

_____

13. How can having a diverse workforce be a benefit to a company?

_____

_____

14. How can having a diverse workforce be a challenge to a company?

_____

_____

Chapter 2 Diversity and Ethics

C. Ethics and Communication

Directions: Write a *T* in the space provided if the statement is true. Write an *F* in the space if the statement is false.

_____ 1. Ethics are principles of right and wrong.

_____ 2. Some people do not have a set of personal ethics.

_____ 3. Businesses may publish a code of ethics to be followed by employees.

_____ 4. Lying to customers or withholding facts from them is always unethical, but these practices are rarely illegal.

_____ 5. Companies and their employees have an obligation to tell the truth to employees and customers.

_____ 6. When dealing with clients, employees should not overstate claims for products.

_____ 7. Confidential information is private, secret information that is not to be shared with anyone except those authorized to know it.

_____ 8. Stealing a credit card number and using it illegally is an example of identity theft.

_____ 9. Employees should share trade secrets freely with friends in other companies.

_____ 10. Plagiarism is an ethical practice.

_____ 11. Avoiding plagiarism when writing a research report is almost impossible.

_____ 12. Copyright is the legal right of someone, usually the author or artist, to use or reproduce a work.

_____ 13. The rules for what constitutes fair use of copyrighted material are vague.

_____ 14. Copyright protection of a work lasts many years.

_____ 15. Employees should be protective of confidential data stored on computers and networks.

D. Personal Space

Directions:

1. Conduct an experiment to determine how people react when you invade their personal space. Stand several inches closer than you normally would as you talk to various people, including family members, acquaintances, store clerks, instructors, and so on. Do not tell anyone you are conducting an experiment. Observe people's reactions. Do they back away? Do they hold their ground? Are you able to converse normally, or are they distracted by your closeness?

2. After you observe at least five different people's reactions, write a brief article for a newspaper column called "In the Workplace." In the column, remind readers how important it is to respect coworkers' personal space. At the same time, point out that different people need different amounts of personal space, sometimes because of their ethnic or cultural background. Give advice for how to respond to someone who seems to be invading your personal space.

E. Privacy Policies

Companies that sell products online collect personal data, such as addresses and credit card numbers, from customers. Some companies keep customer data strictly private. Some companies give or sell customer names and addresses to other companies. Consumers should learn how their private data will be used before entering it and buying online.

Directions:

1. Work with a classmate to complete this activity.

2. Access the Internet. Go to the sites of two businesses that sell products online.

3. Find and read the privacy policy on each site, which should tell how personal data collected from customers will be used.

4. Write a summary of your findings. For each site, include the following information.

   - Business name

   - Site address

   - Types of products sold by the business

   - Main points of the privacy policy that relate to how customer data may be used

   - Whether or not you would want to enter your data on this site and why

   Site 1

   _____

   _____

   _____

   _____

   _____

   _____

   _____

   _____

   Site 2

   _____

   _____

   _____

   _____

   _____

   _____

   _____

   _____

F. Cross-Cultural Communication

Directions: Read the two situations that follow. Explain what might be done to solve the cross-cultural communication problems. You may need to do research about cultures or business customs before you write your responses.

Situation 1

Brad is a confident owner of a small but growing company. He prides himself on his successful business and its casual atmosphere. He likes to joke that he is the only company president who has never worn a suit to work.

Brad has just finished several days of meetings with four people from a Mexican firm that has expressed interest in marketing his products in Mexico. On the first day, Brad got right down to business. He enthusiastically presented all his products and his entire marketing plan to his guests. He handed out papers, showed graphs and charts, and drew pictures on a flip chart.

On the second day, when it was time for the Mexicans to present their marketing plan, Brad sat back in his chair with his hands locked behind his head.

Now, after the third day, the Mexicans seem eager to return home. They are noncommittal about the proposed deal. Brad fears he has lost his Mexican market.

Write a message to Brad, giving your thoughts as to why the Mexican executives may not want to do business with him.

_____

_____

_____

_____

_____

_____

_____

_____

_____

_____

_____

_____

Situation 2

Diane Black is a competent, helpful, and respected member of a newspaper staff. She happens to be the only Jewish person on the staff. The newspaper's editor, John Dempsey, is aware that the newspaper's audience is becoming more culturally diverse. For that reason, he is running more stories with a multicultural slant to them.

Whenever John has a story idea about a topic that is non-Christian, or if someone needs to interview a non-Christian, he gives that story to Diane. He figures she will do a good job because she is not Christian.

Around the newspaper office, everyone is friendly. In December, there is always a big office Christmas party that everyone attends. Last year, Diane suggested tactfully that it be called a holiday party, rather than a Christmas party. At first, John was embarrassed. Later, though, he figured Diane could just deal with it. Certainly, she had been around people who celebrate Christmas all her life. What difference does it make what the party is called? The party is always held in mid-December close to Christmas. The timing just works out that way.

Write a message to Diane's boss, John Dempsey, pointing out why his treatment of and attitude toward Diane are inappropriate.

_____

_____

_____

_____

_____

_____

_____

_____

_____

_____

_____

_____

_____

_____

_____

_____

_____

_____

Chapter 3
Nonverbal Communication and Teamwork

A. Key Terms

Directions: Write the letter of the definition that matches the word beside each word.

_____	1. active listening	a.	Messages sent without or in addition to words
_____	2. casual listening	b.	The nearby area around a person or the area the person considers his or her territory
_____	3. evaluative listening	c.	Nonverbal cues, such as voice pitch, rate of speech, laughing, and sighing
_____	4. nonverbal communication	d.	Hearing and understanding a message but not trying to remember the message in the long term
_____	5. paralanguage	e.	The interaction of people or things that creates or accomplishes more than the sum of the individual efforts or parts
_____	6. personal space	f.	Hearing and trying to understand and remember a message
_____	7. synergy	g.	Two or more people acting together to achieve a goal
_____	8. teamwork	h.	Hearing and judging the importance or accuracy of what a speaker is saying

B. Nonverbal Communication

Directions: Answer each question in the space provided.

1. List two types of cues contained in written and spoken communication.

   _____

   _____

2. What are the four roles of nonverbal communication?

   _____

   _____

   _____

   _____

3. Give an example of how a nonverbal cue can substitute for a verbal message.

_____

_____

4. How much space is considered appropriate for the following space zones? Give an example of the communication that might occur in each type of zone.

	Space	Examples
Intimate Zone	_____	_____
Personal Zone	_____	_____
Social Zone	_____	_____
Public Zone	_____	_____

5. Give three examples of nonverbal cues that may be used in the environment.

_____

_____

6. How can being too self-confident hinder your communication and hurt your image?

_____

_____

7. How can having too little self-confidence hinder your communication and hurt your image?

_____

_____

8. Give three examples of paralanguage.

_____

_____

9. Give two examples of body language and tell their meanings.

_____

_____

10. What is the most acceptable form of touching in the American business environment?

_____

C. Listening

Directions: Write a *T* in the space provided if the statement is true. Write an *F* in the space if the statement is false.

_____ 1. The listening process involves hearing, focusing attention, understanding, and remembering.

_____ 2. Nonverbal cues cannot add meaning to a message.

_____ 3. Understanding is the first step in the listening process.

_____ 4. Focusing attention is the step in the listening process when the listener detects sounds.

_____ 5. Informative listening is a type of casual listening.

_____ 6. Emphatic listening is a type of active listening.

_____ 7. Listening used to obtain specific information or understand a message is reflective listening.

_____ 8. Evaluative listening involves judging the importance or accuracy of what a speaker is saying.

_____ 9. Parallel talk can help the listener understand the speaker and help the speaker clarify thoughts or feelings.

_____ 10. Critical listening is another name for informative listening.

_____ 11. Attitudes about the speaker or the topic can be a barrier to listening.

_____ 12. Room temperature that is too warm or cool is an example of an assumption that can hinder listening.

_____ 13. The speaker has most of the responsibility for conveying meaning during the communication process.

_____ 14. Feedback can tell the speaker that you are listening and that you understand the message.

_____ 15. To listen effectively, you should listen with an open mind.

D. Listening Strategies

Directions: List ten strategies you can use to become a better listener.

1. _____

2. _____

3. _____

4. _____

5. _____

6. _____

7. _____

8. _____

9. _____

10. _____

E. Listening in a Conference Setting

Directions: List seven guidelines for taking part in a seminar or conference.

1. _____

2. _____

3. _____

4. _____

5. _____

6. _____

7. _____

F. Practice Listening Skills

Directions: Listen to a news report on the radio or television. Make notes as you listen. Answer these questions about the news report.

1. What persons, companies, or groups are mentioned in the report?

   _____

2. What is the main topic of the report?

   _____

3. When did (or will) the event or story take place?

    _____

4. Where did (or will) the event or story happen?

    _____

5. Why is the story or event of interest?

    _____

G. Workplace Relationships

Directions: Answer each question in the space provided.

1. Why is respecting lines of authority in communicating with other employees important for keeping a good relationship with your manager?

    _____

    _____

2. What should you do if you think your manager has asked you to do something that is illegal or unethical?

    _____

    _____

3. Why should you seek feedback on your work from your manager?

    _____

    _____

4. When would it be appropriate to share confidential company information with a coworker? Give an example.

    _____

    _____

5. Give an example of how you could show appreciation or acknowledge good work done by coworkers.

    _____

    _____

H. Teamwork

Directions: Work with four or five other students to complete this activity.

1. Form a team whose task will be to evaluate the quality of school life and recommend changes to improve any shortcomings. List the team member names here. Identify one person as the team leader.

   _____

   _____

2. Changes may include anything from landscaping to general maintenance to fostering a more positive attitude among students. Your team may focus on part or all of the campus. Describe the topic or area your team will address here.

   _____

   _____

3. Meet as a team at least four times during a two-week period. Follow the guidelines given in your textbook for stating the goal of the team, assigning tasks, setting deadlines, and working together.

4. Key a summary of the team's findings and recommendations for changes.

5. After the team has completed its task, evaluate how well the team members worked together. Write a general description of how the team functioned and give suggestions for improvement.

   _____

   _____

   _____

   _____

   _____

   _____

   _____

   _____

   _____

   _____

Chapter 4
Grammar and Sentence Review

A. Key Terms

Directions: Write the letter of the definition that matches the word beside each word.

_____ 1. adjective

_____ 2. adverb

_____ 3. conjunction

_____ 4. interjection

_____ 5. noun

_____ 6. preposition

_____ 7. pronoun

_____ 8. verb

a. A word that names a person, place, or thing

b. A word that describes action or state of being

c. A word that connects nouns or pronouns to other words in a sentence

d. A word that describes a noun or pronoun

e. A word that joins words, phrases, or clauses

f. A word that describes a verb, adjective, or adverb

g. A word that expresses surprise or strong feeling

h. A word that takes the place of a noun

B. Parts of Speech

Directions: Write the following paragraph. Insert words that correspond to the parts of speech indicated in parentheses.

Please give (noun) a copy (preposition) the expense summary you and (pronoun) compiled. Then when you and I (verb) next week, we can look for ways to cut (adjective) expenses. Only by (adverb) reviewing all expenses can we be sure to cut costs (conjunction) increase profits.

_____

_____

_____

_____

_____

_____

_____

_____

C. Simple or Compound Subjects

Directions: Underline the simple or compound subject in each sentence.

1. The two actors with several years of training will be asked to perform.

2. Neither the tellers nor the loan officers understand the directive.

3. The secretaries worked overtime on Monday.

4. Both of the men were late to work.

5. Kareem and Chloe's sister won a merit scholarship.

D. Simple or Compound Predicates

Directions: Underline the simple or compound predicate in each sentence.

1. Each of us has her suit pressed and ready to wear.

2. The employees have listened carefully and have heeded our advice.

3. Some parts of the report are concise and clear.

4. The residents will scrape the walls and woodwork before painting them.

5. Careful reading, studying both the characters and the plot, enhances reading enjoyment.

E. Simple, Compound, and Complex Sentences

Directions: Indicate whether the sentence is simple, compound, or complex in structure in the space provided below each sentence.

1. Being nervous can cause an applicant to interview poorly.

   _____

2. Because she did not have all the information, she could not complete the form.

   _____

3. I saw your advertisement for a person with good communication skills.

   _____

4. Please consider me an applicant for this position.

   _____

5. The report is not finished, and the meeting will be postponed.

   _____

6. The new order forms have arrived, and they should last about three months.

   _____

7. When purchasing a new appliance, consider features and cost of the item.

   _____

F. Plural Nouns

Most noun plurals may be formed by using one of the following three rules.

1. Add *s* to the end of most nouns to form the plural.

	Singular	Plural
Common Nouns	pamphlet	pamphlets
	employee	employees
Proper Nouns	Smith	the Smiths
	Corvettes	Corvettes
Abbreviations	CPA	CPAs

2. Add *es* to a singular noun that ends in *s, x, z, sh,* or *ch.*

	Singular	Plural
Common Nouns	lens	lenses
	tax	taxes
	wrench	wrenches
Proper Nouns	Lynch	the Lynches
	Lopez	the Lopezes

3. Add an *s* to form the plural of nouns ending in *y* when the *y* follows a vowel (*a, e, i, o,* or *u*). To form the plural of common nouns that have a consonant (all letters except vowels) before the final *y,* change the final *y* to *i* and then add *es.*

	Singular	Plural
Y after a Vowel	delay	delays
	tray	trays
Y after a Consonant	city	cities
	territory	territories

Directions: Write the plural of each noun. Check a dictionary if you are not sure how to form the plural.

	Singular	Plural
1.	book	_____
2.	lass	_____
3.	radio	_____
4.	facility	_____
5.	coach	_____
6.	activity	_____
7.	Perez	_____
8.	RN	_____
9.	x-ray	_____

G. Proper and Common Nouns

Directions: In each sentence, underline the proper nouns once and the common nouns twice.

1. The two clerks are working in the Silverman Building.

2. Every workstation is connected by the network to our server.

3. The photographer, Amy Cordova, submitted all the photos.

4. Star Company distributes products for several different companies in Tennessee.

5. Frank approved all the layouts, but the president of the company has not seen them.

6. One judge announced her retirement for early next year.

H. Pronouns: Who and Whom

Knowing when to use *who* and *whom* puzzles many writers. Follow these guidelines that can help eliminate any questions about using *who* or *whom* in your writing and speaking.

1. Use the nominative form *who* when the subject of a verb is needed. If you can substitute other nominative case pronouns such as *he, she, we,* or *they,* then *who* is the correct choice.

    Who should attend? (*He/She* should attend.)

2. Use the nominative form *who* as a predicate nominative.

    She is *who?* (*She* is my stepmother.)
    The leaders are *who?* (The leaders are *they.*)

3. Use the objective form *whom* as the direct object of a transitive verb. If you can substitute other objective case pronouns such as *him, her, them,* or *me,* then *whom* is the correct choice.

    Talia selected *whom?* (Talia selected *him.*)
    Whom did Demarcus call this morning? (Demarcus called *them* this morning.)

4. Use the objective form *whom* as the object of a preposition.

    To *whom* should I give the key? (I should give the key to *him.*)
    The donation is for *whom?* (The donation is for *them.*)

Whoever is the nominative form and follows the same guidelines as *who. Whomever* is the objective form and follows the same guidelines as *whom.*

Directions: Underline the correct pronoun in each sentence.

1. (Whoever/Whomever) answers the telephone will win a prize.

2. For (who/whom) should I write the report?

3. Where is the man (who/whom) we saw last night?

4. We will answer to (whoever/whomever) the committee chooses.

5. Give the books to (whoever/whomever) she suggests.

6. (Who/Whom) will go with me?

I. Using Adverbs Correctly

Some adverbs are often used incorrectly by writers. Read the following guidelines for using these words correctly.

Bad or Badly   The adjective *bad* follows the linking verbs *feel* and *look*.
Don't feel *bad* about your absence. He looks *bad*.

The adverb *badly* describes how something is done.
Luann behaved *badly*. Curt plays ball *badly*.

Never or Not   Use *never* when you mean *not ever*.
I have *never* skied. They have *never* been late for rehearsals.

Use *not* in short-term negative situations.
I have *not* skied since Monday. They have *not* been late recently.

Real or Really   *Real,* an adjective, means *genuine*.
This is a *real* diamond. He testified that the brooch is a *real* antique.

Really, an adverb, means *actually*.
Did you *really* see him? Mr. Stearns *really* enjoys substitute teaching.

Sure or Surely   *Sure,* an adjective, means *certain* or *positive*.
Small retailers are *sure* to be on the mailing list.

Surely, an adverb, means *certainly*.
Surely, you can understand our logic.

Good or Well   *Good,* always used as an adjective, means *suitable* or *praiseworthy*.
She told the group the *good* news.

Well, usually used as an adverb, tells how something is done. *Well* also is used as an adjective when referring to health.
He communicates *well* with others. Carey doesn't feel *well* today.

Directions: Underline the correct word in each sentence.

1. Scott felt (well/good) about taking part in the event.

2. Mr. Salo was (sure/surely) pleased with the test results.

3. Ms. Williams is a (real/really) good player.

4. We are pleased to hear you are feeling (well/good) after your surgery.

5. I feel (bad, badly) about their loss in the playoffs.

6. I have (never, not) eaten sushi.

7. She has (never, not) arrived yet.

8. James is the first to admit he plays the guitar (bad/badly).

J. Using Prepositions Correctly

Some prepositions are often used incorrectly by writers. By observing the following guidelines, you can avoid errors in your writing.

Between or Among The preposition *between* is used to connect two nouns or pronouns to the rest of a sentence. The preposition *among* is used to connect three or more nouns or pronouns to the rest of a sentence.

> *Between* Nan and Bruce, who is the better tennis player?

> *Among* Maria, Nan, and Bruce, who is the best tennis player?

In or Into The preposition *in* refers to position. The preposition *into* refers to motion or movement.

> After Isabella walked *into* the store, she looked for a salesclerk *in* the shoe department.

> While Sayid was working *in* the lab, he was called *into* Brad's office for a meeting.

Like or As The preposition *like* requires an object. The conjunction *as,* which is used to introduce a clause, does not require an object. *Like* and *as* cannot be used interchangeably.

> The firm plans to buy a sheet-fed press just *like* its other one.

> We hope to hire another employee *like* Lisa.

> Recite the poem *as* it appears in your book.

> *As* your instructor suggested, check each step carefully.

Beside or Besides The preposition *beside* means *next to*. It is not interchangeable with the preposition *besides,* which means *in addition to.*

> Set the package *beside* the one on the floor.

> The dog sits *beside* the empty food bowl every morning.

> No one *besides* Denver was willing to agree to the terms of the contract.

> *Besides* that, what else is new?

Directions: Underline the correct word in each sentence.

1. The fruit was divided (between/among) the four children.

2. Jan walked (in/into) the room.

3. The coat is (in/into) the closet.

4. She wanted to buy a coat (like/as) the one Mary has.

5. Write your name (beside/besides) mine.

6. (Between/Among) apples and oranges, which one do you want?

7. (Like/As) I was crossing the street, I saw my friend.

8. Where will you go (beside/besides) the Grand Canyon?

Chapter 5
Mechanics of Writing

A. Types of Sentences

Directions: Identify each sentence as a declarative sentence, a mild command, an indirect question, or a courteous request.

1. Watch what you say around the office.

   _____

2. Would you please grant me an extension.

   _____

3. Business law is my favorite course this semester.

   _____

4. Please plan to work overtime on Saturday to help take inventory.

   _____

5. They asked whether you would be able to decorate the gym.

   _____

B. Periods and Question Marks

Directions: Circle the correct punctuation mark at the end of each sentence.

1. Mr. Rich asked when the furnace was last serviced (. / ?)

2. Would you please give me an opportunity to speak with you about my qualifications (. / ?)

3. Do you know that a big price difference exists between London broil and flank steak (. / ?)

4. Where is your agent now? in Florida? in Alabama? in Puerto Rico (. / ?)

5. I would appreciate your not asking me that question (. / ?)

6. May I request you call me before the week is over (. / ?)

7. Do you really think this topic is appropriate for our audience (. / ?)

8. You bought all of the ingredients, didn't you (. / ?)

9. Watch out (! / .) Here comes a foul ball (! / ?)

10. Stop it (! / .) Don't ever do that again (. / ?)

C. Commas

Directions: Insert and delete commas in the sentences as needed.

1. I will go to the store, and buy the ingredients.
2. While driving home from the interview she thought about the job offer.
3. Yes I will consider attending the seminar.
4. Personally I believe we should wait at least two weeks.
5. Listening carefully, is important in this situation.
6. Next winter regardless of my schedule we will go skiing.
7. Katherine Turner who is a newscaster thoroughly enjoys her work.
8. Your earning a scholarship Rudy is a credit to your family.
9. The couch is modern comfortable and attractive.
10. She moved to 10 State Road Dayton Ohio last Saturday.
11. Once before he stated, he wanted to go.
12. The interviewer judges the personality, appearance etc. of each candidate.
13. That restaurant serves a big big breakfast every Sunday morning.
14. They have more than 1000 bags of used clothes stored in the warehouse.
15. After all you have accomplished more than anyone else I know.
16. Jada is not sure, Dr. Thorn when she can meet with you.

D. Identifying Comma Use

Directions: Identify the specific comma use in each sentence.

1. We have no place to stock 1,000 soft pretzels for the fair.

   _____

2. They sold Julius the vase; Bertha, the set of tables; and Antique Masters, the twin lamps.

   _____

3. The well-educated, enthusiastic applicant was hired.

   _____

4. My supervisor, Barnett Davis, has good management skills.

   _____

5. Jocelyn and Donovan served a salad, spaghetti, and iced tea.

   _____

6. We can't thank you enough, Mr. Cohen, for your assistance.

   _____

E. Semicolons

Directions: Insert and delete semicolons in the sentences as needed.

1. The staff members profited by attending the in-service session however, it set them back one week in meeting their quota.

2. The computer is in the second-floor office suite the answering machine is in the reception area.

3. People who own cars must have auto insurance; and should carry their owner's card.

4. You, Dina, should drive carefully in winter weather for instance, be prepared for changing conditions, respect the winter weather, and know how to react to trouble.

5. The 2006 World Cup soccer games were held in Germany a match between France and Sweden took place on June 13 in Stuttgart.

6. The mechanic worked several hours on my car however, it still does not run smoothly.

7. Kiko faxed the order to the deli it was never received.

8. My itinerary includes places such as Key West, Florida Savannah, Georgia and Charleston, South Carolina.

9. Terri and Cory suggested some convenient dates to consider for example, January 2, February 28, or April 15.

10. In April, we get a lot of rain but in August, we get nothing but hot, dry weather.

F. Colons

Directions: Insert colons in the sentences as needed.

1. The skills needed for model railroading are these working with electricity, building models, and using small tools.

2. The list of items includes the following

    1. Paper plates and napkins

    2. Paper cups and 10 two-liter bottles of soda

    3. Three paper tablecloths and six bags of ice

3. In the article, the author stated "It is a wonder that in just ten years, a small town has become such a thriving and successful medium-size city because of the entertainment and casino business."

4. The garden is beautiful The flowers are abundant, and the bushes are trimmed to perfection.

5. Bonita awakens at 615 to take the 730 subway to work.

6. Four colors are acceptable pale green, shell, cream, and soft, pale yellow.

G. Dashes

Directions: Insert dashes in the sentences as needed.

1. Amanda has intelligence and maturity two traits that contribute to her success.

2. Good management skills, effective listening habits, and patience those are the qualities of a good manager.

3. Three of our brightest graduates Becca, Manuel, and Nathen will address their classmates at tomorrow's assembly.

4. Dillon Flaherty he's the one who moved from Boise is our ace.

5. Renee disapproves of the design change but, of course, Renee always disagrees with my decisions.

H. Hyphens

Directions: Insert hyphens in the sentences as needed.

1. Her attorney at law is Sam Duncan, a graduate of Harvard.

2. Trevor's father in law was the founder of the company.

3. I like Mazie's down to earth attitude.

4. The self made entrepreneur is proud of her success.

5. She is the ex president of the local auxiliary.

I. Quotation Marks

Directions: Insert quotation marks and commas in the sentences as needed.

1. They each get an allowance said Meg. He spends it wisely, but she squanders it.

2. Clancy stated The firefighters had yelled Leave the building at once!

3. We believe said Connie and Chandler that the school should be co-ed.

4. After scanning the article on testing, did they say, This will never work?

5. Genevieve inquired Are you going on safari in Kenya?

J. Parentheses

Directions: Insert parentheses in the sentences as needed.

1. Irina or Marv one or the other will most likely be selected.

2. We saw many couples six we knew on the boardwalk.

3. In the article on photography May issue of *Photography Digest*, our new camera was featured.

4. The price of General Motors GM stock may be attractive to investors.

5. Before leaving, you should a) lock the file cabinet, b) turn off the lights, and c) lock the door.

K. Apostrophes

Directions: Insert apostrophes in the sentences as needed.

1. The stadium project represents three years labor.

2. "The *t*s are purposely left uncrossed," said Beryl.

3. Their companys profits went up during the first quarter of 05.

4. Its a very long commute to the office.

5. My father-in-laws loan subsidized Ellens car purchase.

L. Abbreviations

Directions: Insert abbreviations as needed and spell out words that should not be abbreviated.

1. Miss Grace Bright and Mister Ronald Key will be our delegates.

2. Doctor Douglas Fox is a noted cardiologist in Land City.

3. Lana Grayson, Certified Public Accountant, is auditing the books this week.

4. On what rd. did you say the Kosars live?

5. Dr. Goldman's new address is 16 Pine Blvd. Northwest.

6. The receptionist comes from either WY or WV; I can't remember which one.

7. Does Ofelia live on Tustin St. or Tustin Rd.?

8. My mailing address is 15 Aruba Drive, Lafayette, Louisiana 70507-3142.

M. Capitalization

Directions: Correct errors in capitalization in the sentences.

1. let me tell you what i learned from the experience.

2. Rafael asked, "will the meeting begin soon?"

3. the movie *the creature from the Deep* is too scary for children.

4. The president's residence, the White House, is not open to tourists today.

5. The building on the corner is the seacrest inn.

6. Students study the declaration of independence at holmes junior high school.

7. When you go to paris, buy some french perfume.

8. Our family dines together on thanksgiving day.

9. My favorite building in new york is the empire state building.

10. She is a linguist; she speaks spanish, italian, and german fluently.

N. Number Usage

Directions: Select the correct number usage in the sentences.

1. Eva usually travels to Duluth (4 / four) times a year.

2. The volunteers distributed approximately (200 / two hundred) meals on Thanksgiving.

3. Please bring (57 / fifty-seven) twelve-foot boards to the building site.

4. (15 / Fifteen) local businesses participated in Career Day.

5. Antonia completed her remodeling project on (1/23/18 / January 23, 2018).

6. Please mail your reservation form by April (4 / 4th).

7. While on the island, I stayed at (One / 1) Sunburst Place.

8. If I had ($1,000,000 / $1 million), I would share it with you.

9. The conference call will begin at (eleven-thirty o'clock / 11:30) a.m.

10. More than (two-thirds / 2/3) of the sales agents will attend the sales meeting.

Chapter 6
The Writing Process

A. Key Terms

Directions: Write the letter of the definition that matches the word beside each word.

_____	1.	bias	a.	The process of correcting grammar and spelling in a piece of writing
_____	2.	editing	b.	Reviewing and correcting the final draft of a message
_____	3.	empathy	c.	A belief or opinion that hinders fair and impartial actions or judgments
_____	4.	intranet	d.	A word or phrase used to connect one idea to the next
_____	5.	proofreading	e.	Needlessly repetitive
_____	6.	publish	f.	Understanding of another's feelings or point of view
_____	7.	redundant	g.	Send a message to a receiver or make a message available to a receiver
_____	8.	transition	h.	A communications network within an organization that is meant for the use of its employees or members

B. Planning and Organizing Messages

Directions: Answer each question in the space provided.

1. What are the five steps in the writing process?

    _____

    _____

2. What four steps are involved in planning a message?

    _____

    _____

    _____

    _____

3. What is goodwill? Why is it important for a business?

_____

_____

4. A business message should accomplish one or more of five basic objectives. What are these objectives?

_____

_____

_____

5. How can you determine the objective of a business message you are writing?

_____

_____

6. Which parts of a message should be identified first—the main idea or the supporting details? Why?

_____

_____

7. List three or more questions you can answer to help you adjust your message to the receiver.

_____

_____

_____

_____

8. What types of messages should be written using direct order? With direct order, where is the main idea presented?

_____

_____

9. What types of messages should be written using indirect order? With indirect order, where is the main idea presented?

_____

_____

10. When should direct-indirect order be used for a message?

_____

C. Composing Messages

Directions: Write a *T* in the space provided if the statement is true. Write an *F* in the space if the statement is false.

_____ 1. Concise messages show respect for the reader's time.

_____ 2. Courteous messages show the biases of the writer.

_____ 3. Negative messages should not be written in a positive tone because this will confuse the reader.

_____ 4. Use a person's title and last name in a business message when you want to show respect.

_____ 5. Courteous messages do not make the receiver feel singled out in a negative way.

_____ 6. The word *policeman* shows gender bias.

_____ 7. The word *salesperson* shows gender bias.

_____ 8. Gender-specific pronouns should be used to refer to neutral nouns.

_____ 9. Writers should avoid biases of race and age by not mentioning race or age unless it is essential to the message.

_____ 10. Messages that contain errors create a negative impression of the writer.

_____ 11. Correctness is not important in routine messages to coworkers.

_____ 12. Concise messages do not contain unrelated material that can distract the reader from the important points of the message.

_____ 13. Redundancies, empty phrases, and unneeded words weaken business messages.

_____ 14. When you write in the active voice, the subject of the sentence receives the action of the verb.

_____ 15. Clear messages do not contain contradictory information.

_____ 16. Complete messages contain all the information needed to achieve the objectives of the sender.

_____ 17. A business message that includes the five Ws (who, what, where, when, and why) cannot be concise.

_____ 18. A topic sentence states the main idea of a paragraph.

_____ 19. A complete business message typically has opening, developmental, and closing paragraphs.

_____ 20. The closing paragraph of a business message may summarize the message or refer to the main idea stated in the opening paragraph.

D. Editing and Proofreading Messages

Directions: Write the letter of the correct answer beside each number.

_____ 1. Reviewing and revising a message to improve it is

      a. proofreading
      b. editing
      c. composing

_____ 2. A word or phrase that connects sentences in paragraphs is

      a. a preposition
      b. an omission
      c. a transition

_____ 3. Writers can indicate changes to be made

      a. using proofreaders' marks or a software feature, such as Track Changes
      b. using software features such as spell-check and grammar-check
      c. using brainstorming methods

_____ 4. Reviewing and correcting the final draft of a message is

      a. proofreading
      b. editing
      c. composing

_____ 5. When you use a spelling and grammar checker

      a. all errors will be found by the program
      b. some errors will be found by the program
      c. only misspelled words will be found by the program

_____ 6. The proofreaders' mark that appears as a wavy line beneath a word indicates that the word

      a. should appear in bold type
      b. should be underlined
      c. should be deleted

_____ 7. The proofreaders' mark that appears as three short horizontal lines beneath a letter indicates that the letter

      a. should appear in bold type
      b. should be capitalized
      c. should be deleted

_____ 8. The proofreaders' mark that appears as dots beneath a word and is shown with the letters _stet_ indicates that

      a. the word should appear on a separate line
      b. the marked correction should not be made
      c. the words should be transposed

E. Proofreading Methods

Directions: List six methods for proofreading business documents.

1. _____

2. _____

3. _____

4. _____

5. _____

6. _____

F. Publishing Messages

Directions: List one or more appropriate methods for publishing the message described.

1. A message to your supervisor that contains your comments on an employee's work performance

   _____

2. A draft of a report on which you want team members to comment

   _____

3. A message to an important client regarding an ongoing project

   _____

4. An announcement to all employees from management regarding a change in when payroll checks will be issued

   _____

5. A reply to a routine email from a coworker

   _____

G. *You*-Oriented Messages

A *you*-oriented message focuses on what the receiver wants or needs to know rather than on the writer's needs. This writing style is often called the *you* approach. The tone of a *you*-oriented message tells the receiver that he or she is the focus of the message.

You-Oriented	I-Oriented
Welcome to the Tech Advantage customer family. Come in and use your Tech credit card soon.	I am pleased to inform you that your Tech credit card has been approved. I hope you visit us soon.
Your order will be shipped on July 1. Thank you for ordering from us.	I am sorry, but I can't ship your order until July 1. The items you want are out of stock.

Directions: Rewrite each message to use the *you* approach.

1. I cannot send your package until August 10. We won't have the items until then.

   _____

   _____

   _____

2. The software problem cannot be resolved until the virus is removed. I suggest that you install a current version of an antivirus program.

   _____

   _____

   _____

3. We are happy to inform you that your warranty has not expired. I can send you a check to cover the cost of repairing the appliance after I get a receipt showing the repair cost.

   _____

   _____

   _____

4. I need more details before I can send the information you requested. I need to know the year and the state in which each transaction took place.

   _____

   _____

   _____

Chapter 7
Writing Memos, Email, and Letters

A. Key Terms

Directions: Write the letter of the definition that matches the word beside each word.

_____	1.	body	a.	An informal message written, sent, and received on a computer, smartphone, or electronic tablet
_____	2.	email	b.	A format style that has a colon after the salutation and a comma after the complimentary close in a letter
_____	3.	flame	c.	An informal document sent to someone within your organization
_____	4.	memo	d.	A format style with no punctuation after the salutation or complimentary close in a letter
_____	5.	mixed punctuation	e.	An angry or insulting email message
_____	6.	netiquette	f.	Unsolicited electronic junk messages
_____	7.	open punctuation	g.	A set of informal guidelines for behaving courteously online
_____	8.	spam	h.	The part of a document (memo, email, or letter) containing the paragraphs of the message

B. Business Correspondence

Directions: Answer each question in the space provided.

1. What are three examples of business correspondence?

   _____

   _____

2. Which types of business correspondence might be sent by interoffice mail?

   _____

   _____

3. Which document is considered more formal—a letter, a memo, or an email message?

   _____

   _____

4. When might a letter be sent to someone inside the organization?

_____

_____

5. What information is typically included in a company letterhead?

_____

_____

6. What is the purpose of an invoice?

_____

_____

7. What are six purposes for which a document might be written?

_____

_____

_____

_____

_____

_____

8. What are the four steps in the process of planning a message?

_____

_____

_____

_____

9. What order should be used to write a positive or a neutral message?

_____

_____

10. What order should be used to write a negative or a persuasive message?

_____

_____

C. Memos, Emails, and Letters

Directions: Write a *T* in the space provided if the statement is true. Write an *F* in the space if the statement is false.

_____ 1. A memo has three lines in the heading.

_____ 2. Side margins for a memo should be 2.5 inches.

_____ 3. The top margin for a memo should be about 2 inches.

_____ 4. The paragraphs in the body of a memo should be double-spaced.

_____ 5. A copy notation is used to indicate that someone other than the primary recipient will receive a copy of the document.

_____ 6. An enclosure notation is used to indicate that something is attached to the document.

_____ 7. Using a distribution list for a memo is appropriate when the memo is being sent to two people.

_____ 8. The subject line of a document states the main idea or topic of the message.

_____ 9. The first line in the paragraphs of a memo should be indented 1 inch.

_____ 10. Bulleted or numbered lists may be used in memos and letters to present details clearly.

_____ 11. Tables and charts should not be used in the body of a memo.

_____ 12. You should include reference initials only on memos or letters you key for someone else.

_____ 13. When a memo or letter requires more than one page, a heading should appear on all pages after the first page.

_____ 14. Publishing a memo is typically accomplished by placing it in an envelope and sending it by interoffice mail.

_____ 15. A vague subject line may cause an email message to be ignored or deleted as spam.

_____ 16. You do not need to check the size of an email file attachment because all email systems can handle large attachments.

_____ 17. When you compose an email message, you can choose an address from the address book instead of keying the address.

_____ 18. You should select the Draft option when you are ready to send an email message.

_____ 19. In modified block letter style, all lines begin at the left margin.

_____ 20. An attention line is used when a letter is not addressed personally to an individual, but rather to an organization.

D. Netiquette

Directions: Write the letter of the correct answer beside each number.

_____ 1. Netiquette

    a. is a set of informal guidelines for behaving courteously online.

    b. is important only when communicating for work—not with personal messages.

    c. is important only when sending personal messages—not for communicating for work.

_____ 2. You should assign a high priority to an email message

    a. only when the message is truly urgent.

    b. routinely, so all your messages will be read.

    c. only if you suspect the receiver will ignore the message.

_____ 3. When you want to send a file attachment with an email message

    a. you need not ask the recipient first.

    b. you should ask the recipient first if the file is large.

    c. you should always ask the recipient first.

_____ 4. Unsolicited email messages, called spam,

    a. should be sent only to close friends or colleagues.

    b. should never be forwarded to others.

    c. should be sent only by professional advertising companies.

_____ 5. Confidential or sensitive information

    a. is best sent by email because email is fast.

    b. is best sent by email because email is private and secure.

    c. should not be sent by email because email is not secure.

_____ 6. When keying an email message

    a. do not use emoticons in business messages.

    b. some errors are acceptable because the message is informal.

    c. use all capital letters to get the reader's attention.

_____ 7. An email flame

    a. is an angry or insulting message.

    b. should never be sent to a coworker.

    c. both a and b

_____ 8. Using informal abbreviations, such as *TTYL* for *talk to you later,* in an email message

    a. is acceptable.

    b. is not acceptable.

    c. may be acceptable, depending on who the recipient is.

E. Document Formats

Directions: Answer each question in the space provided.

1. What top and side margins should be used for a memo?

    _____

2. What top and side margins should be used for a letter?

    _____

3. How should the paragraphs in the body of a letter or memo be keyed?

    _____

4. How is the format of a block letter different from the format of a modified block letter?

    _____

5. What information is included in the second page heading for a memo or letter?

    _____

F. Compose an Email Message

Directions

1. Assume that you are an instructor at a community college. Write a brief email to the college registrar, Joan Radford. Use an address supplied by your instructor (or make up an address and do not actually send the message but save it as a draft). Use an appropriate subject line.

2. In the email body, ask when the schedule of classes for the next semester will be announced. In addition, ask about any changes in the policy on cancelling courses.

G. Key a Memo

Directions: Key the text shown below in proper memo format. Add an appropriate notation.

TO: Willis Langtree | FROM: Sandra Lee | DATE: Current Date | SUBJECT: Increased Production

The attached document summarizes suggestions from the members of my department. These suggestions may increase line production by as much as 35 percent. Please let me know when we can meet to discuss these ideas.

Thank you for giving our department members the opportunity to contribute ideas for improving our work processes.

H. Key a Letter

Directions: Key the text shown below in proper block letter format. Use open punctuation. Assume the letter will be printed on letterhead paper. Prepare an envelope (or paper cut to envelope size) for the letter. Assume that the envelope will have a preprinted return address.

January 15, 20--

Ms. Iris Watkins
14 Cooper Road
Niles, IL 60714-7635

Dear Ms. Watkins

Your appointment on Monday, January 23, at the Spivey Center is confirmed. At this visit, you will begin your six-week rehabilitative program. Your therapy will take place from 10:00 a.m. to noon on Mondays, Wednesdays, and Fridays. Please arrive at 9:45 a.m. on your first day. Present this letter and the enclosed permission form to the receptionist in the main lobby.

If you have any questions, please contact my assistant, Rachel Waters, at 555-0124. We look forward to working with you to help you recover from your injury. Your personal therapist will work closely with you to develop a program that meets your needs.

Sincerely

Patrice Nye
Director, Physical Therapy

xx

Enclosure

Chapter 8
Writing to Clients and Customers

A. Key Terms

Directions: Write the letter of the definition that matches the word beside each word.

_____ 1. acknowledgment

a. A message that requests a refund, an exchange, or a discount on merchandise or services

_____ 2. claim

b. A request that the receiver sell goods or services to the sender

_____ 3. collection message

c. A message that tells a sender that a message or item has been received

_____ 4. goodwill message

d. A formal document that describes a problem or need and recommends a solution

_____ 5. order

e. A message that asks for information or action that the sender thinks will be given or done willingly

_____ 6. proposal

f. A friendly message designed to build relationships

_____ 7. routine request

g. A message that tries to persuade a potential customer to purchase a product or service

_____ 8. sales message

h. A message that tries to persuade a customer to pay a past-due bill

B. Neutral and Positive Messages

Directions: Answer each question in the space provided.

1. What are the four steps in planning a business message?

_____

_____

_____

_____

2. In what order should messages with positive or neutral news be organized?

_____

_____

3. Where should the main idea appear in messages with positive or neutral news? Where should the supporting details appear?

_____

_____

4. What is a soft sell message? Where should it appear when included in a letter?

_____

_____

5. Where should the main idea appear in a routine request letter?

_____

_____

6. What is the purpose of a claim message?

_____

_____

7. What information should be provided for items in an order?

_____

_____

_____

_____

_____

_____

8. What order should be used for writing a positive response to a request?

_____

9. Give three examples of messages that may be expressed in a goodwill letter.

_____

_____

10. What is the purpose of an acknowledgment message?

_____

C. Negative Messages

Directions: Write a *T* in the space provided if the statement is true. Write an *F* in the space if the statement is false.

_____ 1. A negative message conveys news that will disappoint the receiver.

_____ 2. Maintaining goodwill is not important in negative messages.

_____ 3. People from some cultures may view a writer's use of concise writing as somewhat short and abrupt.

_____ 4. The tone of a negative message should reflect a sincere concern for the receiver's interests.

_____ 5. A negative message should simply state the bad news; it should not include reasons for the bad news.

_____ 6. Messages with negative news should be organized in an indirect order.

_____ 7. Negative messages should begin with a neutral opening.

_____ 8. In a negative message, the bad news should be stated in the first paragraph.

_____ 9. The supporting details in a negative-news message provide the reasons for the negative news.

_____ 10. In the closing of a message containing negative news, do not mention or remind the receiver of the negative news again.

D. Persuasive Messages

Directions: Write the letter of the correct answer beside each number.

_____ 1. A message that tries to convince the reader to take an action is a

    a. routine request.
    b. persuasive message.
    c. positive news message.

_____ 2. The main idea in a persuasive message should

    a. show that the requested action will benefit the receiver.
    b. give information that will convince the receiver to do as you request.
    c. consider the reader's concerns and probable reaction to the request.

_____ 3. A persuasive message

    a. should be organized in direct order.
    b. should state the main idea in the last paragraph.
    c. should be organized in indirect order.

_____ 4. The last paragraph in a persuasive message should

    a. ask for a specific action.
    b. provide supporting details.
    c. give an apology to the reader.

_____ 5. An obstacle
   a. is something that hinders or prevents progress or achieving a goal.
   b. is often related to a lack of time or money.
   c. both a and b

_____ 6. A primary appeal
   a. is not needed in a persuasive message.
   b. is the most convincing point in a persuasive message.
   c. is presented in the first paragraph of a persuasive message.

_____ 7. A request for specific action
   a. is given in the last paragraph of a persuasive message.
   b. is given in the first paragraph of a persuasive message.
   c. should be as vague as possible.

_____ 8. For collection messages
   a. the urgency stage is the first stage.
   b. the urgency stage is the last stage.
   c. the discussion stage is the first stage.

_____ 9. A proposal
   a. is a formal document that describes a problem and recommends a solution.
   b. is a formal document that describes a problem but does not recommend a solution.
   c. is always solicited.

_____ 10. In a proposal
   a. the background section is optional.
   b. an action plan is not usually included.
   c. the need or problem is described at the end.

E. Types of Letters

Directions: Indicate the type of letter each sentence might open.

1. The brochures you ordered are enclosed.

   _____

2. Please send me the items listed below.

   _____

3. Please send me information about your health club.

   _____

4. Your new charge account has been approved.

   _____

5. The toaster, which I purchased from your online store, does not heat properly.

   _____

F. Review a Message

Directions: Read the message below and then answer the related questions.

Dear Mr. Watson

A new rugby shirt is being sent to you today. You made an excellent choice when selecting this shirt, but two rules for washing must be followed carefully:

1. The shirt must be washed in cold water.

2. No bleach should be used when washing it.

If you send the shirt to a laundry, be sure to give the clerk these directions. When directions are followed, the shirt will provide the excellent wear you seek.

During next week, April 13-20, new, wrinkle-free cotton shirts will be reduced 30 percent. Come in and see them.

1. What type of letter is this?

   _____

2. In what order is the letter written?

   _____

3. What is the objective of the message?

   _____

4. What is the main idea of the message?

   _____

5. What are the supporting details?

   _____

   _____

6. Is the closing appropriate? Why or why not?

   _____

   _____

7. Is the letter *you* oriented?

   _____

8. How could the letter be improved?

   _____

   _____

   _____

G. Edit Negative News Statements

Directions: Rewrite the following statements to soften the negative news. Use the technique indicated.

Use an "If" Clause

1. I can't attend the sales meeting because I will be in Chicago at a conference on computer development.

   _____

   _____

2. Because of the budgetary constraints in our department, I cannot let you purchase new furniture for your office.

   _____

   _____

Use Passive Voice

3. We cannot reserve a room for you at the hotel where the conference is being held. We have reserved a room for you at the Salter Hotel instead.

   _____

   _____

4. Because of the amount of artwork to be done, we won't have the advertising campaign ready on schedule. It won't be ready until May 19.

   _____

   _____

Indicate What You Can Do

5. I'm sorry; we won't be able to send your personal computer until May 15.

   _____

   _____

6. Because of scheduling difficulties, I won't arrive in New Orleans until 7 p.m. on Thursday.

   _____

   _____

7. We will not be able to extend a loan to you until you improve your credit score.

   _____

   _____

Chapter 9
Writing Reports

A. Key Terms

Directions: Write the letter of the definition that matches the word beside each word.

_____   1.   analytical report   a.   A list of sources used in preparing a report or other written work

_____   2.   appendix   b.   A set of questions used to learn facts or opinions

_____   3.   bibliography   c.   A listing of topics in a logical order

_____   4.   executive summary   d.   Supplementary materials that are placed at the end of a document or book

_____   5.   outline   e.   A list of what is included in a report, book, or other document

_____   6.   scope   f.   A synopsis or an abstract of a report

_____   7.   survey   g.   The boundaries of the report

_____   8.   table of contents   h.   A report that analyzes a problem, presents facts and conclusions, and makes recommendations

B. Planning Reports

Directions: Answer the questions in the space provided.

1. How do formal reports differ from informal reports?

     _____

     _____

     _____

     _____

     _____

2. How do analytical reports differ from informational reports?

     _____

     _____

     _____

     _____

3. Informal reports may be formatted in what three ways?

_____

_____

_____

4. What steps are involved in planning a report?

_____

_____

_____

_____

_____

_____

5. What is a report timeline? How do you go about creating a report timeline?

_____

_____

_____

_____

6. How does secondary research differ from primary research for a report?

_____

_____

_____

_____

7. What are three ways to gather data when doing primary research?

_____

_____

_____

8. List three types of printed resources you can use to find data for creating a report.

_____

_____

9. List the steps used to find information using a search engine.

_____

_____

_____

_____

_____

_____

_____

_____

10. List some questions you can ask yourself to help evaluate data from secondary sources.

_____

_____

_____

_____

_____

C. Bibliography and Research Notes

Directions: Answer the questions in the space provided.

1. What information should be included on a bibliography note for material from a book? Give an example bibliography note for a book.

_____

_____

_____

_____

2. What information should be included on a bibliography note for material from a magazine or journal article? Give an example bibliography note for a magazine or journal article.

_____

_____

_____

_____

_____

3. What information should be included on a bibliography note for material from a web page? Give an example bibliography note for a web page.

_____

_____

_____

_____

_____

4. What information should be included on a research note?

_____

_____

_____

D. Report Outlines

Directions: Answer the questions in the space provided.

1. List five ways in which the outline for an informal report may be organized.

_____

_____

_____

_____

_____

2. What is a hypothesis? How can hypotheses be used in a report outline?

_____

_____

_____

_____

_____

3. How does an alternative that may be used in a report outline differ from a hypothesis?

_____

_____

4. Follow these steps to create a report outline:

- Identify a club or sports event for your school with which you are familiar. For example, you might select soccer games as the event.

- Assume that attendance has been low at the past several events. Create two or three hypotheses that might explain why attendance has been low. For example, one hypothesis could be that the soccer games have been scheduled at the same time as another popular school event, which takes away attendance from the games. Another hypothesis could be that the weather has been cold and rainy for the last few games, causing attendance to be low.

- Working from your hypotheses, create an outline for a report that addresses the issue of low attendance. Under each hypothesis, list the questions that must be answered to prove or disprove the hypothesis.

_____

_____

_____

_____

_____

_____

_____

_____

_____

_____

_____

5. A discussion outline is shown on the left below. On the right, rewrite the outline as a topical outline.

Discussion Outline	**Topical Outline**
I. The first step in planning a report is identifying the problem.	_____
A. The writer must decide on areas to investigate.	_____
B. The writer must determine the scope of the report.	_____
C. The writer must identify limitations of the report.	_____
II. The writer must gather data for the report.	_____
A. The writer must decide how to collect data.	_____
B. The writer must complete the data gathering.	_____

E. Report Organization and Style

Directions: Answer the questions in the space provided.

1. What is the main idea in an informational report?

   _____

   _____

2. What is the main idea in an analytical report?

   _____

   _____

3. When should you use direct order for a report?

   _____

   _____

4. When should you use indirect order for a report?

   _____

   _____

5. Why is an impersonal writing style typically used for formal reports?

   _____

   _____

F. Report Timeline

Directions: You work in the Human Resources Department of a large retail store. Your manager has asked you to create a short customer satisfaction survey and report. Details of the project are given below.

- The survey will be completed by randomly selected customers as they exit the store.
- You and two other employees (whom you will train) will ask the survey questions.
- The survey will be completed over a three-day holiday weekend (Saturday through Monday). (Assume a three-day holiday weekend falls within the time period given.)
- You will then compile the data and present the results in a report to your manager.
- You have six weeks from today to design the survey, train the two employees, conduct the research, compile the data, and write the report.

Prepare a timeline to plan and schedule each phase of this project. Create the timeline using spreadsheet or word processing software.

Chapter 10
Graphics and Visual Aids

A. Key Terms

Directions: Write the letter of the definition that matches the word beside each word.

_____	1. bar chart	a.	An image that shows a step-by-step diagram of a procedure or process
_____	2. clip art	b.	An image that shows the relationships of employees, positions, and departments
_____	3. flowchart	c.	An image that shows changes in quantity or value over time
_____	4. legend	d.	An image that shows how the parts of a whole are distributed
_____	5. line chart	e.	An image used to compare amounts in one or more categories
_____	6. organization chart	f.	A chart feature that identifies the items that the pieces, columns, bars, or lines in the chart represent
_____	7. pie chart	g.	An arrangement of data organized in rows and columns
_____	8. table	h.	A drawing or image that has been saved as an electronic file

B. Using Graphics and Visual Aids

Directions: Answer each question in the space provided.

1. What are four examples of visual aids?

   _____

   _____

   _____

   _____

2. How are the terms *visual aid* and *graphic* related?

   _____

   _____

3. Give one reason that communicators are using more visual aids than in the past.

_____

_____

4. How can you decide where to place a visual aid in a document?

_____

_____

5. What does "referencing a graphic" mean?

_____

_____

6. For what purpose is clip art typically used in a document?

_____

_____

7. Describe a numbering system that could be used for charts when several appear in two or more sections of a document.

_____

_____

_____

_____

_____

_____

8. What information should be included in the source line for a chart or table? Give an example source line.

_____

_____

_____

_____

_____

C. Visual Aid Uses

Directions: Write a *T* in the space provided if the statement is true. Write an *F* in the space if the statement is false.

_____ 1. Tables show exact figures or present detailed information in an organized, easy-to-follow format.

_____ 2. A line chart shows lines of authority and relationships among employees or job positions.

_____ 3. A pie chart illustrates the steps in a procedure or process.

_____ 4. A flowchart shows how the parts of a whole are distributed.

_____ 5. Bar charts show a comparison of amounts.

_____ 6. Column charts show a comparison of amounts.

_____ 7. A pie chart shows how the parts of a whole are distributed.

_____ 8. Drawings show a realistic view of an item, person, or place.

_____ 9. Maps show geographic regions such as cities, states, or countries.

_____ 10. Drawings are clip art or line art images that add interest or show specific details of an object.

D. Developing Graphics

Directions: Answer each question in the space provided.

1. Name three types of software that can be used to create visual aids.

   _____

2. What is the purpose of *Word's* Table Styles gallery?

   _____

   _____

3. List six guidelines for creating effective tables.

   _____

   _____

   _____

   _____

   _____

   _____

   _____

4. What do solid lines in an organization chart show? What do dotted lines show?

_____

5. What is the purpose of a chart legend?

_____

E. Create a Pie Chart

Directions: Create a pie chart to show the distribution of grades in a Business Communication class.

1. For the chart title, key BUSINESS COMMUNICATION GRADES.

2. The grades assigned in the Business Communication class are shown below.

A	25%
B	20%
C	40%
D	10%
F	5%

3. Include a chart legend.

4. Show values on the pie chart pieces.

5. Print the chart.

F. Create a Line Chart

Directions: Create a line chart to show changes in stock prices for two stocks.

1. For the chart title, key STOCK PRICES.

2. The years and the end-of-year stock prices for each stock are shown below.

Year	Ace Products	Wilson Tools
2008	75	83
2007	80	78
2006	65	75
2005	63	77
2004	60	79

3. Use a different color for each line and include a chart legend.

4. Label the vertical axis **Price in Dollars**.

5. Show values on the data points.

6. Print the chart.

G. Create a Column Chart

Directions: Create a column chart to compare overtime hours worked in three departments.

1. For the chart title, key OVERTIME FOR MAY.

2. The departments and the overtime hours worked for one month for each department are shown below.

Department	May Overtime Hours
Sales	56
Marketing	62
Human Resources	47

3. Label the vertical axis **Overtime Hours.**

4. Show values on the columns.

5. Print the chart.

H. Create a Flowchart

Directions

1. Identify a process for which you will create a flowchart. For example, you could create a chart to show the process of scanning an image to a file.

2. Identify a name for the process.

3. Identify the steps in the process, decision points, data input or output points, and documents that may be created as part of the process.

4. Identify an appropriate flowchart symbol to use for item in the flowchart.

5. Create the flowchart. Include a title that identifies the process.

6. Use an appropriate flowchart symbol for each item in the chart. Use color effectively to make the chart easy to follow.

7. Print the chart.

I. Letter with Table

Directions: Key the handwritten letter below in block format. Use open punctuation. Assume the letter will be printed on letterhead paper. Use an attractive format for the table. Center the table horizontally.

January 15, 20--

Ms. Iris Watkins
14 Cooper Road
Niles, IL 60714-7635

Dear Ms. Watkins

Thank you for requesting a schedule of classes available at our community center during June. Some classes are open only to adults. Others are open to children, who should be accompanied by an adult. The class schedule is shown in the table below.

CLASS	OPEN TO	DATE	FEE
Beginning Swimming	Adults	June 2	$10
Finger Painting Fun	Children	June 5	5
Swimming for Toddlers	Children Ages 2 and 3	June 7	10
Quilting Basics	Adults	June 5	10

Class times and materials needed are listed in the attached brochure. If you have any questions, please contact me for more information.

Sincerely

Patrice Nye, Director

Attachment

Chapter 11
Technical Communication

A. Key Terms

Directions: Write the letter of the definition that matches the word beside each word.

_____ 1. description   a. A detailed listing of the topics and subtopics covered in a book, manual, or other written work

_____ 2. glossary   b. Sets of instructions combined with explanations, descriptions, definitions, and other related information

_____ 3. index   c. A verbal and/or visual picture of something

_____ 4. instructions   d. A series of events that take place over time and result in a change or a product

_____ 5. manuals   e. A list of terms and abbreviations with definitions

_____ 6. object   f. Writing specific, detailed instructions and descriptions

_____ 7. process   g. Something inanimate that is natural or synthetic and can be seen or touched

_____ 8. technical writing   h. Steps that tell readers how to do something

B. Writing Instructions

Directions: Answer each question in the space provided.

1. What parts are included in effective instructions?

   _____
   _____
   _____
   _____

2. How do the terms *instructions* and *manuals* relate to each other?

   _____
   _____
   _____
   _____

3. What information should be included in the introduction for a set of instructions?

_____

_____

_____

_____

_____

_____

_____

_____

4. What is the primary goal when writing steps for instructions?

_____

_____

5. What are three guidelines that apply to all technical writing?

_____

_____

_____

6. When a set of instructions has many steps, how should they be arranged?

_____

_____

7. What is *white space* in a document? Why should you use ample white space when writing instructions?

_____

_____

8. How should warnings be treated in a set of instructions?

_____

_____

_____

_____

9. What questions can you ask as you edit instructions to help you improve them?

_____

_____

_____

_____

_____

10. Why is it important to work through the steps when editing instructions?

_____

_____

C. Effective Manuals

Directions: Write a *T* in the space provided if the statement is true. Write an *F* in the space if the statement is false.

_____ 1. An effective manual has a broad, nonspecific title.

_____ 2. An effective manual has a detailed table of contents.

_____ 3. Manuals often combine sets of instructions for completing various tasks with statements of policies or procedures.

_____ 4. The introduction to a manual should explain how the manual is organized, how it can be used and by whom, and what processes or procedures it covers.

_____ 5. Manuals are typically not divided into sections or chapters.

_____ 6. Tables are typically not used in manuals.

_____ 7. Manuals should use illustrations wherever they would be helpful to readers.

_____ 8. A manual may have an index, which is a list of terms and abbreviations with definitions.

_____ 9. A manual might include an appendix with supplemental material at the end of the manual.

_____ 10. Several features of word processing software can help users create manuals efficiently.

_____ 11. The table of contents for a manual should include page numbers to make it easy for readers to locate specific topics.

_____ 12. Figures and charts should not be listed in the table of contents of a manual.

D. Writing Descriptions

Directions: Answer each question in the space provided.

1. How does a set of instructions differ from a process description?

   _____

   _____

2. What parts are included in an effective object description?

   _____

   _____

   _____

3. What parts are included in an effective process description?

   _____

   _____

   _____

4. What is included in the body of an object description? A process description?

   _____

   _____

   _____

   _____

   _____

   _____

5. What should the introduction for a process description include?

   _____

   _____

   _____

6. When should the writer use present tense for writing a process description? Past tense?

   _____

   _____

E. Write a Process Description

Directions:

1. Obtain permission from a worker or classroom instructor to observe a process, such as how a plumber makes a solder joint or how a hairstylist applies highlights.

2. Write a description of the process based on your observations. Your audience is an adult who has never performed the process.

3. Make sure your description includes a title, an introduction and overview, a step-by-step description, and a conclusion.

4. Print the process description, and ask the person to evaluate your description for accuracy.

5. Make corrections using the person's evaluation and print a final copy of the process description.

F. Write Instructions for a Task

Directions:

1. Select a task for which you will write instructions, such as baking a cake or placing new strings on a guitar.

2. Write instructions for the task. Your audience for the instructions is your classmates.

3. Make sure your instructions include a title, an introduction and list of items or skills needed, step-by-step directions, warnings (if needed), and a conclusion.

4. Ask a classmate to read the instructions and provide suggestions for improvement.

5. Make corrections using the feedback and print a final copy of the instructions.

G. Edit Instructions

Directions:

1. Read the instructions on the following page. Edit the instructions to:
   - Make the title more specific.
   - Begin all steps with a verb.
   - Correct any errors in spelling, punctuation, grammar, or number usage.
   - Place explanations below steps without numbers.
   - Treat warnings appropriately.

2. Key the instructions, making the edits you have marked.

3. Proofread the instructions and correct all errors. Print the instructions.

Potatoes

Introduction

Potatoes are a favorite food for many people. Growing potatoes requires time, but the results are well worth the effort. The growing time for potatoes is from three to four months. Potatoes should be planted in early spring about a month before the last frost is expected.

Five steps are involved in growing potatoes: prepare the soil, prepare the seed potatoes, plant the seed potatoes, care for the plants, and harvset the crop. You will need the following tools and supplies: hoe, spading fork, rake, knife, water, seed potatoes, and fertilizer.

Soil Preparation and Planting

Follow these steps to prepare the soil and plant potatoes:

1. Clear the garden spot of debris.
2. Select a garden spot with loam soil.
3. Digging holes that are about 3 to 5 inches deep comes next. The holes should be 12 to 15 inches apart.
4. Cut the seed potatoes into small pieces, making sure each piece has at least one eye.
5. Place a piece of seed potato in each hole.
6. Fill the each hole, placing 3 to 5 inches of soil over each seed potato.
7. Water after filling the holes and applying fertizler.
8. Apply commercial fertilizer according to package directions. Be careful to keep fertilizer away from pets and children. It can be poisonous if swallowed.

Plant Care and Harvesting

Follow these steps to care for the potato plants as they grow and to harvest the potatoes:

1. As the plants grow, weed the plants and water them if rainfall is not plentiful.
2. Apply fertilizer regularly according to the package directions.
3. Spary or dust with insecticide if insects begin to eat the plant tops. Be careful to keep insecticide away from pets and children. It can be poisonous if swallowed.
4. Allow the potatoes to dry completely before storing.
5. Dig very carefully to remove potatoes from the ground at harvest time.

Conclusion

Potatoes should be stored in a dark, cool place that has good air circulation. They should remiain fresh and ready for you to eat and enjoy for several months.

Chapter 12
Technology in the Workplace

A. Key Terms

Directions: Write the letter of the definition that matches the term beside each term.

_____	1.	compact disk (CD)	a.	The study of the relationship between people and their working environment
_____	2.	computer virus	b.	A person who uses computer expertise to break into computer networks
_____	3.	ergonomics	c.	A group of devices, such as computers and printers, connected together in order to share data and/or tasks
_____	4.	firewall	d.	A thin platter that can have computer data recorded on it in optical form
_____	5.	hacker	e.	A digital phone service in which calls go through a high-speed Internet connection rather than a conventional phone line
_____	6.	hotspots	f.	A device that combines the features of a cell phone and a handheld computer
_____	7.	network	g.	A computerized system that answers telephone calls
_____	8.	smart phone	h.	A program that can infect data files or programs without the knowledge of the user
_____	9.	voice mail	i.	Places that offer wireless Internet access
_____	10.	VoIP	j.	Hardware and/or software that restricts access to computers or networks

B. Technology at Work

Directions: Answer each question in the space provided.

1. What does the term *technology* mean?

   _____

   _____

   _____

2. What are the physical parts of a computer called?

   _____

   _____

3. What type of personal computer fits on a desk but is too large to carry easily from place to place?

    _____

    _____

4. What does a laptop computer have in common with a desktop computer? How are they different?

    _____

    _____

    _____

5. What are the advantages of a tablet computer over a laptop computer?

    _____

    _____

    _____

6. What does a handheld computer have in common with a tablet computer? How are they different?

    _____

    _____

    _____

    _____

7. Give three examples of application software.

    _____

    _____

8. What is the function of operating system software?

    _____

    _____

    _____

    _____

9. What is the purpose of utility software?

    _____

    _____

C. File Storage and Management

Directions: Write a *T* in the space provided if the statement is true. Write an *F* in the space if the statement is false.

_____ 1. There is no need to back up computer files you create at work.

_____ 2. A compact disk (CD) can store more data than a digital video disk (DVD).

_____ 3. To use CD-Rs and CD-RWs, your computer must have a special drive used to read and save data to CDs.

_____ 4. A flash memory device can keep stored information without needing a power source.

_____ 5. Flash memory is used in a variety of appliances, including cell phones, video games, music players, and video cameras, but not for saving computer data.

_____ 6. File compression software can be used to reduce the size of a file.

_____ 7. You should use meaningful names for your computer files and be consistent in how you name files.

_____ 8. You can move, copy, and delete files but not folders.

_____ 9. The Search feature can be used to find files by name, type, date created, and text within the file.

_____ 10. A folder created on a computer storage media can contain files and other folders.

D. Peripherals

Directions: Write the letter of the correct answer beside each number.

_____ 1. Printers, scanners, and fax machines are common

   a. computer peripherals.
   b. storage options.
   c. computer software applications.

_____ 2. The newest printer technology uses

   a. ink cartridges to produce an image on a page.
   b. toner cartridges to produce an image on a page.
   c. plastic to create three-dimensional items.

_____ 3. A machine that creates a computer file from a paper copy, slide, or film is a
   a. printer.
   b. GPS unit.
   c. scanner.

_____ 4. Some scanners work with optical recognition software (OCR)
   a. that change color pages to black and white pages.
   b. that "read" the page and allow the scanned text to be edited.
   c. to enlarge or reduce images.

5. A device that sends and receives electronic documents over a phone line is a

   a. scanner.
   b. printer.
   c. fax machine.

6. A computerized system that answers telephone calls is

   a. voice mail.
   b. GPS.
   c. VoIP.

7. A portable, wireless telephone that changes antenna connections during travel from one radio reception cell to another is called a

   a. VoIP.
   b. cell phone.
   c. GPS.

8. A device that combines the features of a handheld computer with those of a cell phone is a

   a. scanner.
   b. GPS.
   c. smart phone.

9. A device that records images in digital form on a sensor chip instead of film is a

   a. digital camera.
   b. fax.
   c. VoIP.

E. Workplace Safety

Directions: Answer each question in the space provided.

1. What government agency has as its main goal promoting the safety and health of American workers?

   _____

2. What are five causes of accidents and injuries in offices?

   _____
   _____
   _____
   _____
   _____

3. List five examples of how to be safety-conscious at work.

_____

_____

_____

_____

_____

F. Communication Barriers

Directions: Read the two cases and answer the questions in the space provided.

Case A

Madalena is a nurse practitioner at a hospital. Her work includes patient interviews. She enters a patient's room, sets up her laptop, greets the patient, and starts keying. Madalena does not look up very often while entering data because she does not want to make a mistake. She speaks quickly because she has many patients to see.

1. How do you think Madalena's way of working makes patients feel?

_____

_____

_____

_____

_____

2. What advice would you give Madalena for communicating better with patients?

_____

_____

_____

_____

_____

Case B

The lights in the conference room went down, but the light on the cell phone of the woman next to you did not. It looks as though she plans to send text messages throughout the entire presentation. You find the light and activity distracting and her behavior rude. Judging from the expressions of the people around you, they do too.

3. Have you been in a situation where another person's use of a cell phone or pager was distracting or annoying? Describe the situation.

_____

_____

_____

4. If you are in a situation such as the one described here, what can you do or say to let the person know tactfully that he or she is distracting others?

_____

_____

_____

G. Review a Voice Mail System

Directions:

1. Choose an organization that uses an automated telephone answering system.

2. Call the organization and listen carefully. Call as many times as necessary to navigate the entire system (without talking with a person). As you listen, take notes in the space provided below.

3. Key a short paper describing the system and making recommendations for improvements. Include a chart showing all or some of the navigation system.

_____

_____

_____

_____

_____

_____

_____

_____

_____

Chapter 13
Presentations and Meetings

A. Key Terms

Directions: Write the letter of the definition that matches the term beside each term.

_____	1. agenda	a.	Characteristics of a group of people, such as gender, age, race, culture, education level, occupation, and income
_____	2. brainstorming	b.	Work with other people to accomplish a task
_____	3. briefing	c.	The official record of the proceedings of a meeting
_____	4. collaborate	d.	Thinking of many ideas about a topic without evaluating the ideas
_____	5. demographics	e.	An outline that uses a few words to describe each topic rather than complete sentences
_____	6. impromptu speech	f.	A speech in which computer software is used to combine several kinds of visual and/or audio aids
_____	7. minutes	g.	A document that lists the topics to be discussed during a meeting
_____	8. multimedia presentation	h.	A group charged with completing a specific job within a certain time
_____	9. task force	i.	A short, informal talk given with little advance notice or preparation
_____	10. topical	j.	A short presentation given to bring people up to date on business activities, projects, programs, or procedures

B. Oral Presentations

Directions: Answer each question in the space provided.

1. What kind of information should you include when introducing a speaker?

   _____

   _____

   _____

   _____

2. What is the purpose of a briefing?

_____

_____

3. What are the steps in planning a formal presentation?

_____

_____

_____

_____

_____

4. When planning a presentation, why it is important to analyze the audience?

_____

_____

_____

_____

5. What is the most effective mode (way) of delivery for a speech?

_____

_____

6. How does an impromptu speech differ from a formal presentation?

_____

_____

_____

_____

7. What are five attention-getting techniques you might use to open a speech?

_____

_____

_____

_____

_____

8. What should you do to prepare for the question-and-answer portion of a presentation?

    _____

    _____

9. What are four types of nonverbal cues that may be used during an oral presentation?

    _____

    _____

    _____

    _____

10. Why is feedback during and after a presentation important to the presenter?

    _____

    _____

C. Visual Aids

Directions: Write a *T* in the space provided if the statement is true. Write an *F* in the space if the statement is false.

_____   1. Effective use of visual aids can make speakers appear more credible than speakers who did not use visuals aids.

_____   2. Posters can be prepared ahead of time to use as visual aids during a presentation.

_____   3. A multimedia presentation can include features such as sound and animation.

_____   4. An electronic whiteboard can scan text and images written on it and send the images to a computer or printer.

_____   5. A handout distributed at the end of a presentation can be used to supply reference materials for your audience to use later.

_____   6. The equipment available is not a consideration when deciding on the type of visual aids to use for a presentation.

_____   7. You should use the visual aids that are easiest for you to create regardless of audience needs.

_____   8. No matter how long a speech is, not more than ten visual aids should be used.

_____   9. Practicing a speech using your visual aids is not usually necessary.

_____   10. When using visual aids, you should face the screen rather than the audience.

D. Meeting Documents

Directions: Write the letter of the correct answer beside each number.

_____ 1. A document that lists the topics to be discussed during a meeting is

   a.   an agenda.
   b.   an itinerary.
   c.   action minutes.

_____ 2. An agenda includes

   a.   a list of topics to be discussed.
   b.   the name of the person who will lead the discussion for each topic.
   c.   both a and b

_____ 3. The official record of the proceedings of a meeting is called

   a.   an agenda.
   b.   an itinerary.
   c.   minutes.

_____ 4. Action minutes

   a.   summarize topics discussed and decisions made.
   b.   list actions to be taken.
   c.   both a and b

_____ 5. A document that can be used by the meeting leader to keep the meeting on track is

   a.   minutes.
   b.   an agenda.
   c.   an itinerary.

E. Taking Part in Meetings

Directions: Answer each question in the space provided.

1. What can you do to prepare to take part before a meeting?

   _____

   _____

   _____

2. What steps can you take to be sure you arrive at an offsite meeting on time?

   _____

   _____

   _____

3. List five things you can do to make a positive impact at a meeting.

_____

_____

_____

_____

_____

4. What strategies can you use to handle difficult people when you are the meeting leader?

_____

_____

_____

_____

5. What should the meeting leader do to end the meeting appropriately?

_____

_____

_____

F. Presentation Fears

Directions: Read the case below and answer the questions in the space provided.

Sam Turney impressed his small audiences as a volunteer speaker for Memorial Hospital. Sam thought his presentations were effective. Still, he was delightfully surprised when Susanna Marguiles, the patient relations director, offered to hire him as a full-time member of her staff.

Susanna wants Sam to expand his talks to include groups of all sizes and presentations on a variety of health themes. Susanna also wants Sam to begin using presentation software and equipment. Sam is anxious because he feels more comfortable with small groups. He knows little about presentation software and equipment.

Susanna helps Sam with his first electronic presentation. However, Susanna will be attending a conference in another city when Sam gives his second talk. It will be a presentation before an audience of hundreds. The goal of the talk is to persuade parents to take child CPR classes.

Sam is terrified as he prepares his presentation. He feels a little better after Susanna calls to give him advice. "You're using the same strong communications skills," she told him, "even if the audience is larger and the equipment is more sophisticated."

1. What tips or advice can you give Sam for planning the presentation?

   _____

   _____

   _____

   _____

   _____

2. What tips or advice can you give Sam for planning the visual aids for his speech?

   _____

   _____

   _____

   _____

   _____

3. What tips or advice can you give Sam for delivering the presentation?

   _____

   _____

   _____

   _____

   _____

   _____

G. Team Presentation

Directions:

1. Work with two classmates to plan and prepare a speech. Your audience will be your classmates. The speech should take 5 to 7 minutes to deliver.

2. Identify a topic and ask your teacher to approve it.

3. Working with your classmates, do research on the topic and create a topical outline.

4. Plan and create appropriate visual aids.

5. Decide who will present each part of the speech. Practice as a group and using the visual aids.

6. Deliver the speech to the class or a group of classmates.

Chapter 14
Verbal Communication with Customers

A. Key Terms

Directions: Write the letter of the definition that matches the term beside each term.

_____	1. credibility	a.	The sound of your voice that incorporates pitch, quality, and strength
_____	2. customer service	b.	The property of a sound, such as a voice, that describes it as high or low
_____	3. enunciation	c.	An online discussion group that focuses on a specific topic
_____	4. external customer	d.	An employee of your company to whom you provide information or services
_____	5. internal customer	e.	Someone from outside the organization who receives benefits or information or purchases a product or service
_____	6. newsgroup	f.	The way in which each part of a word is said
_____	7. pitch	g.	The performance of activities to ensure customer satisfaction
_____	8. tone	h.	The quality of being believable or trustworthy

B. Customer Service

Directions: Answer each question in the space provided.

1. Give one example of an internal customer and one example of an external customer.

   _____

   _____

   _____

2. What does it mean to be accessible to customers?

   _____

   _____

   _____

3. Why do you need to be aware of your company's policies in order to provide good customer service?

_____

_____

_____

4. How can you be sure you are giving knowledgeable responses to customers' questions?

_____

_____

5. What guidelines can you follow to use email effectively for customer service?

_____

_____

_____

_____

_____

_____

_____

_____

6. List five characteristics of a customer-friendly website.

_____

_____

_____

_____

7. What can you do to make a good first impression on customers?

_____

_____

_____

_____

8. What can you do to deal ethically with customers?

_____

_____

_____

_____

9. Why is it important to determine a customer's needs?

_____

_____

_____

10. What does the phrase "match the solution to the problem" mean? Give an example.

_____

_____

_____

C. Face-to-Face Communication

Directions: Write a *T* in the space provided if the statement is true. Write an *F* in the space if the statement is false.

_____ 1. Most of us prefer to listen to voices that are neither too high nor too low in pitch.

_____ 2. Your listeners may think you lack confidence if you speak too quietly.

_____ 3. The tone of your voice may be the voice quality customers remember the most.

_____ 4. Speakers have no control over the tone of voice they use.

_____ 5. Poor enunciation makes your speech difficult to understand.

_____ 6. Saying "nuc q ler" instead of "noo kle er" is an example of incorrect pronunciation of the word *nuclear*.

_____ 7. The exchange is the part of a conversation that happens first.

_____ 8. The closing to a business conversation should always be formal.

_____ 9. When you meet new customers, you should use their surnames, particularly if they are older than you.

_____ 10. Making eye contact is not important when talking with customers.

_____ 11. You should be courteous in your speech, even if a customer becomes unpleasant.

_____ 12. Building trust is not important in relationships with customers.

D. Telephone Communication

Directions: Answer each question in the space provided.

1. List two advantages to communicating with customers by telephone.

   _____

   _____

   _____

2. How can you show courtesy for others when talking on a cell phone in a public place?

   _____

   _____

   _____

3. What should you do if a caller becomes abusive or uses profanity?

   _____

   _____

   _____

4. Why is it important to observe verbal cues when talking on the phone with a customer?

   _____

   _____

   _____

5. What are five activities involved in planning an outgoing call?

   _____

   _____

   _____

   _____

   _____

6. What should you do when you reach the recipient of your outgoing call?

   _____

   _____

   _____

7. Why is it not a good idea to leave lengthy voice mail messages?

_____

_____

8. What information should you give a caller when you need to transfer the call?

_____

_____

_____

9. What information should be included in a telephone message that you take for a coworker?

_____

_____

_____

_____

_____

_____

10. What information should you try to learn when you screen calls for a coworker?

_____

_____

E. Voice Mail Greeting

Directions: You work in the Accounting Department of Jones and Waters Company. You are in the office today, but you have several meetings that will take you away from your desk at various times. Compose an appropriate voice mail greeting that will play when you are away from your desk and cannot answer the phone. Make up any needed details.

_____

_____

_____

_____

_____

_____

_____

F. Treating Customers Ethically

Directions: Read the case below and answer the questions in the space provided.

A washing-machine service technician evaluates a customer's machine and finds that some of the electrical wiring near the motor is damaged from a flood in the customer's basement. He does not have the needed parts on hand, and replacing the wiring is tedious work. He reports to the customer that the whole motor assembly needs to be replaced.

1. Is the service technician considering the customer's needs? Why or why not?

_____

_____

2. Is the service technician treating the customer in an ethical manner? Why or why not?

_____

_____

G. Customer Service Message

Directions:

1. Read the case below.
2. Key a telephone script that Kevin can use to explain the delay in the delivery of Ms. Cruz's hot rod. Invent any needed details. Include comments Kevin will make and comments the customer may make.

As part of his work toward a Bachelor's Degree in Communications, Kevin Morrissey must complete a summer internship. He had hoped for summer work with a public relations firm or with a company involved in Internet design. However, his advisor strongly suggested an internship with Hot Rods by Boyd.

Kevin soon discovered why his advisor had suggested Hot Rods by Boyd, where customer service really means communication. Much of Boyd's customer service communication is done face-to-face or by telephone.

Unfortunately, because of a fire at a vendor's manufacturing plant, the frames for several Boyd-designed hot rods are late. Several customers' orders will be delayed. Kevin is asked to call these customers and tell them about the delay. Kevin is now on the front line of customer service. Rosetta Cruz is the first customer that Kevin will call with the bad news.

Chapter 15
Employment

A. Key Terms

Directions: Write the letter of the definition that matches the term beside each term.

_____ 1. career portfolio

_____ 2. internship

_____ 3. job interview

_____ 4. career objective

_____ 5. networking

_____ 6. qualifications

_____ 7. reference

_____ 8. résumé

a. An arrangement in which a student works for a company for a set period of time as part of a learning experience

b. Talking with people you know—family, friends, and acquaintances—to locate job openings

c. A computer file, file folder, or notebook containing samples of your work, transcripts, letters of recommendation, and other related items

d. A person who can attest to your character or qualifications for a job

e. A brief statement that describes the type of position an applicant desires

f. A concise summary of an applicant's qualifications for a job

g. A discussion of a job and your qualifications with an employer

h. Skills, abilities, experience, and training that prepare a person to do a job

B. Job Search

Directions: Answer each question in the space provided.

1. Give three examples of questions you can answer to help identify your personal goals.

_____

_____

_____

2. Give three examples of questions you can answer to help identify your career goals.

_____

_____

_____

3. Identify a job and give three examples of your qualifications for that job.

_____

_____

_____

4. What information should you include in your résumé in the work experience section? How can you present this information?

_____

_____

_____

_____

_____

_____

_____

5. When creating a list of your education and training, what information should you include?

_____

_____

_____

_____

6. List five of your personal traits that would help you perform well at work.

_____

_____

_____

_____

_____

7. What samples of work or descriptions of projects can you develop to place in your career portfolio?

_____

_____

_____

_____

C. Résumés

Directions: Write a *T* in the space provided if the statement is true. Write an *F* in the space if the statement is false.

_____ 1. The quality and color of the paper you use for a résumé is not important.

_____ 2. The reader forms a first impression of an applicant based on the appearance of his or her résumé and application letter.

_____ 3. A résumé should contain a summary of the applicant's work experience and education related to the job.

_____ 4. At least three references should be listed on a résumé.

_____ 5. Listing the honors you have received on a résumé is seen as bragging and should be avoided.

_____ 6. Listing a skill on your resume you do not have is acceptable if it helps you get the job.

_____ 7. A résumé can be organized in reverse chronological order or in functional order.

_____ 8. A résumé organized in functional order presents the most recent work experience first and works backward to earlier jobs.

_____ 9. You should not necessarily include a career objective on a résumé.

_____ 10. Employers may be turned off by unprofessional email addresses used on a résumé.

_____ 11. If you are still in school, your education may be your strongest qualification for a job.

_____ 12. On your résumé, it is appropriate to list activities that reflect initiative, leadership, and teamwork skills.

_____ 13. A scannable résumé is one that is delivered in a computer file.

_____ 14. An online résumé is written in HTML and can be viewed on the web using a browser program.

_____ 15. Your electronic résumé should contain the same data as your print résumé.

D. Application Letter and Form

Directions: Answer each question in the space provided.

1. What is the purpose of an application letter? What document should be sent with an application letter?

_____

_____

_____

_____

_____

2. What information should be included in the opening paragraph of an application letter?

_____

_____

_____

3. In what situation would you write an unsolicited application letter?

_____

_____

_____

4. What information should be included in the body paragraph(s) of an application letter?

_____

_____

_____

5. What information should be included in the closing paragraph of an application letter?

_____

_____

_____

_____

6. What is the purpose of an application form?

_____

_____

_____

7. List five guidelines to follow when completing an application form.

_____

_____

_____

_____

_____

_____

Chapter 15 Employment

E. Interview Questions

Directions: Identify a job for which you might apply. Answer the following interview questions as you would in an interview for this job.

Job Position: _____

Questions:

1. What kind of work did you do at your last job?

   _____

   _____

   _____

2. Describe a problem you have had related to your work at school or on a job and tell how you solved the problem.

   _____

   _____

   _____

3. Give an example of how you have worked as part of a team. What did you like about the experience? What did you dislike?

   _____

   _____

   _____

   _____

4. Why do you think you are qualified for this job?

   _____

   _____

   _____

   _____

   _____

5. What salary or wages do you expect for this job? Why do you expect this amount?

   _____

   _____

   _____

   _____

F. Job Opportunities

Directions:

1. Search online to find three good sources of job openings. Give the site name, URL, and a brief description of each site.

   _____
   _____
   _____
   _____
   _____
   _____
   _____
   _____
   _____
   _____

2. Find an employment agency located in your city or area. Give the name of the agency, the address, the telephone number, and the type of jobs for which they find applicants.

   _____
   _____
   _____
   _____
   _____

3. Find a temp agency located in your city or area. Give the name of the agency, the address, the telephone number, and the type of jobs for which they find applicants.

   _____
   _____
   _____
   _____
   _____

Chapter 15 Employment